OLD TESTAMENT READINGS & DEVOTIONALS

Old Testament Readings & Devotionals

VOLUME 11

C.M.H. Koenig

Robert Hawker
Charles H. Spurgeon
Octavius Winslow

C.M.H. Koenig Books

C.M.H. Koenig Books
Copyright © 2021 by Heather L. Rautio

All rights reserved. No part of this book may be reproduced in any manner whatsoever without written permission except in the case of brief quotations embodied in critical articles and reviews.

ISBN 978-1-956475-21-0 (Paperback)
ISBN 978-1-956475-22-7 (eBook)
ISBN 978-1-956475-23-4 (Hardcover)

Scripture quotations, unless otherwise noted, are from the Christian Standard Bible. Copyright © 2017 by Holman Bible Publishers. Used by permission. Christian Standard Bible®, and CSB® are federally registered trademarks of Holman Bible Publishers, all rights reserved.

Scripture quotations marked AKJV are from the Authorized (King James) Version. Rights in the Authorized Version in the United Kingdom are vested in the Crown. Reproduced by permission of the Crown's patentee, Cambridge University Press.

First Printing, 2021

Visit www.cmhkoenigbooks.net

Contents

Preface ix
Compiler's Note xi

1	Reading: Ezra 1	1
2	Reading: Ezra 2	3
3	Reading: Ezra 3	5
4	Reading: Ezra 4	7
5	Reading: Ezra 5	9
6	Reading: Ezra 6	11
7	Reading: Ezra 7	13
8	Reading: Ezra 8	15
9	Reading: Ezra 9	17
10	Reading: Ezra 10	19
11	Reading: Esther 1	21
12	Reading: Esther 2	23
13	Reading: Esther 3	24
14	Reading: Esther 4	26

15	Reading: Esther 5	29
16	Reading: Esther 6	31
17	Reading: Esther 7	33
18	Reading: Esther 8	35
19	Reading: Esther 9	37
20	Reading: Esther 10	39
21	Reading: Nehemiah 1	41
22	Reading: Nehemiah 2	43
23	Reading: Nehemiah 3	45
24	Reading: Nehemiah 4	47
25	Reading: Nehemiah 5	48
26	Reading: Nehemiah 6	50
27	Reading: Nehemiah 7	52
28	Reading: Nehemiah 8	55
29	Reading: Nehemiah 9	57
30	Reading: Nehemiah 10	60
31	Reading: Nehemiah 11	62
32	Reading: Nehemiah 12	63
33	Reading: Nehemiah 13	64
34	Reading: Psalm 126	66
35	Reading: Malachi 1	68
36	Reading: Malachi 2	71
37	Reading: Malachi 3	73

| 38 Reading: Malachi 4 | 75 |

Works Cited | 77
About The Authors | 78

Preface

Old Testament Readings & Devotionals, Volume 11 features Ezra, Esther, Nehemiah, Malachi, and a Psalm. After King Cyrus of Persia's decree to allow Israelites to return to Jerusalem, Ezra records the return of a remnant and rebuilding of the temple in Jerusalem. The book of Esther covers part of King Ahasuerus of Persia's reign, and Queen Esther's saving of the Jewish people. Nehemiah, in his book, recounts the rebuilding of Jerusalem's wall. The book of Malachi reminds us of God's covenant love for his people.

Estimated Timeline: 605 BC – 518 BC

About the series:
The readings and devotionals series compiled by C.M.H. Koenig consists of eleven (11) volumes for the Old Testament and three (3) volumes for the New Testament. They combine a chronological reading plan of the Bible with a related devotional for each "reading." Each reading is generally one chapter and the associated devotionals are excerpts from Robert Hawker (1753–1827), Charles H. Spurgeon (1834-1892), or Octavius Winslow's (1808-1878) works. The Psalms are interspersed throughout the Old Testament volumes.

The intent of the series is to help us savor the scriptures and, in the words of the Psalmist, to "Taste and see that the LORD is good" (Psalm 34:8, CSB).

> *"Charles Spurgeon commended Robert Hawker with these words:"Gentleman, if you want something full of marrow and fatness, cheering to your own hearts by way of comment, and likely to help you in giving your hearers rich expositions, buy Dr. Hawker's Poor Man's Commentary. ... he sees Jesus, and that is a sacred gift, which is most precious whether the owner be a critic or no. There is always such a savor of the Lord Jesus Christ in Dr. Hawker that you cannot read him without profit.""*

Unless otherwise noted, the key verse(s) for each day (in italics) are from the Christian Standard Bible (CSB).

For more information, visit C.M.H. Koenig's website at: www.cmhkoenigbooks.net.

Compiler's Note

Spelling & Grammar:

Some of the spelling has been standardized with modern or American English spelling, such as "traveller" to "traveler," or "neighbour" to "neighbor." All references to "the Holy Ghost" have been standardized to "the Holy Spirit."

Since these writings were taken directly from the authors' original works, there may seem to be some grammatical errors by modern practice. By and large, the grammar remains unchanged from the original text in the cited works.

Scripture References:

The works in this compilation often refer to scripture other than the key verse(s) or scripture reading passage. Some are cited in the original works and others are not. Scripture reference citations contained in the original works as well as additional reference citations added by the compiler are listed at the end of each devotional, as needed, to facilitate cross-reference study. Scripture quoted within the devotionals are direct quotes or paraphrases from the Authorized (King James) Version of the Bible, unless otherwise noted in the original text.

1

Reading: Ezra 1

"King Cyrus also brought out the articles of the LORD's house that Nebuchadnezzar had taken from Jerusalem and had placed in the house of his gods." Ezra 1:7

Was not Cyrus a type, in this instance, of the gentile church, concerning whom it was said that *they should bring of their abundance to beautify the place of God's sanctuary.*[1] And it is remarkable, as if the Lord meant from the earliest days of the church to point out his holy will and pleasure, in making the Jew and Gentile church at length one in Jesus, that in the first wilderness church after the people departed out of Egypt, the church was supplied from the spoils of the Egyptians.[2] But I wish the Reader to make another observation which those verses suggest, namely, amidst all the impiety and profaneness of the kings of Babylon, in desecrating the holy vessels of the temple, how did the Lord watch over both the people and the temple treasures. Yes! the Lord's eye was upon them, and according to his own precious word, their memorial was always before him: *In my wrath I smote thee, saith the Lord; but in my favor have I had mercy* *upon thee.*³ How sweet a lesson this to the long and painful exercises of his afflicted ones now. He knows all they feel; hears every groan; and is speaking to them in the same gracious words; *I the Lord do keep it. I will water it every moment; lest any hurt it, I will keep it night and day.*⁴ (Hawker, Poor Man's Old Testament Commentary: 1 Kings-Esther, 583–584)

Footnotes:
1. Isaiah 60:3–14.
2. Exodus 12:35-36.
3. Isaiah 60:10.
4. Isaiah 27:2-3.

2

Reading: Ezra 2

"These now are the people of the province who came from those captive exiles King Nebuchadnezzar of Babylon had deported to Babylon ..." Ezra 2:1

We are not to suppose that these were individually the very same persons which were carried away and all lived to return. Seventy years must have produced both deaths and births in the several tribes. But I rather conceive, by this register, is meant the exact number of those in each tribe that survived to return.

...No doubt during the captivity a faithful register was kept of the several families, and therefore their number was the more clearly ascertained. Chiefly with an eye to the promised Messiah, each father of the tribe carefully preserved his record. One feature in this record of the families of Israel I cannot help remarking. I mean the smallness of the children of Bethlehem compared to some; —*only* 123. This was what the prophet *Micah* had before noticed. *And thou Bethlehem Ephrathah, though thou be little among the thousands of Judah, yet out of thee shall he come forth unto me that is to be ruler in Israel; whose goings forth have been of old, from everlasting.*[1] What a sweet thought this suggests, not to despise the day of small things! (Hawker, Poor Man's Old Testament Commentary: 1 Kings-Esther, 585, 587)

Footnote:
1. Micah 5:2.

3

Reading: Ezra 3

"When the seventh month arrived ... the people gathered as one in Jerusalem." Ezra 3:1

This seventh month was probably at the time of gathering in their summer fruits. What the country had produced of them is not said. But it was a fit season for assembling upon the great purpose they had in view. I would not have the Reader, methinks, overlook the unanimity which subsisted among them; for we are told they gathered themselves together as one man. Reader! it is this sweet feature of Jesus's gospel which makes both him and his blessed cause so dear. Oneness with him will be sure to make the same with his members. If I love him, I must love my brother that is part of him.[1]

"... began to build the altar of Israel's God in order to offer burnt offerings on it ..." Ezra 3:2

I must beg the Reader very particularly to mark this verse. Here we find that before they begun, or even had power to begin, the foundation for the temple, the altar was set up. Was not this typical of Jesus? Is he not, and was he not ever, the Altar, the Sacrifice, and Priest? What a precious allusion then was this to him, in whom all sacrifices had their substance, and to whom they all referred. (Hawker, Poor Man's Old Testament Commentary: 1 Kings-Esther, 592)

Footnote:
1. John 13:35.

4

Reading: Ezra 4

"Then ceased the work of the house of God." Ezra 4:24 (AKJV)

Ah! how distressed was Zion, when this decree took place. And yet the history of the church plainly proves that the hand of the Lord was in it! My soul, are thine exercises sometimes similar? Doth it seem to thee as if the work of God in thee was at a stand? nay, as if it was totally over? Pause! recollect there is a set time to favor Zion. Thy Jesus is of one mind, and who can turn him? He is everlastingly pursuing the designs of his love. And as Zion was graven upon the palms of his hands, and her walls were continually before him, when she appeared in her most desolate circumstances; so the work of his grace, in the heart of his people, doth not remit, though, to thy view, all thy promising beginnings seem to be blighted, and as it seems in thy apprehension, thou findest growing imperfection. And is not Jesus, by this very means, emptying thee of self, and all the pride of self-attainments? Is he not preparing thee for his own glory, by removing in thee the rubbish of all creature-confidences? Remember what is said; When the Lord shall build up Zion, he shall appear in his glory. Mark here, that it is the Lord that is to build

Zion: and it is the Lord's glory, and not thine, that is to result from it. The work of the house of God in thee would indeed cease, if the work was thine, or thou hadst any hand in the performance of it! But the same almighty hand which laid the foundation of this house, those hands shall also finish it.[1] And by this process, the glorious Builder is teaching thee to cease from thine own works, as Jesus when redemption-work was finished, did from his.[2] Precious Lord! is this the cause, and are these the lessons, thou art teaching me, in the deadness, emptiness, and the numberless complaints under which I daily groan? Oh! then, for grace to cease from self, to cease from all fancied attainments, and to have my whole heart and soul centered in thee, in whom alone is all righteousness, grace, work, and fulness. Yes, Lord! the work is thine, the salvation is thine, the glory is thine, all is thine and all that remains for me, is to be forever giving thee the just praise that is due to thy most holy name, content to be nothing, yea, less than nothing, that the power of Jesus may rest upon me; for when most weak in myself, then am I most strong in the Lord, and in the power of his might. (Hawker, The Poor Man's Morning Portion, May 24)

Footnotes:
1. Philippians1:6.
2. Mark 16:19; Hebrews 12:2.

5

Reading: Ezra 5

The Lord had certainly softened the minds of those men, that though they sent an accusation against the people to the king, yet the Lord overruled the indicting of it. When *a man's ways please the Lord, he maketh even his enemies to be at peace with him.*[1] But I beg the Reader to observe further what confidence the people had taken from the consciousness that the eye of the Lord their God was upon them. No doubt the Lord blessed the words of his servants the prophets unto them. I cannot sufficiently praise the firmness and zeal of the people in stating their just pretensions to prosecute the work; not only because Cyrus the king had tolerated, but from an infinitely higher cause, that the king of kings, even the God of heaven and earth, they were servants to. And they had suffered his displeasure in the captivity they were lately brought out of, for neglecting what they now were determined to engage in. Oh! how precious it is to find souls faithful to God and Christ, and determined to persevere in his service, be the consequence what it may. Reader! make your just observations upon the same characters, as they appeared in the foregoing chapter and in this. *There* through fear of man, which bringeth a snare, they ceased from the work. *Here*, through fear and love of God, which giveth confidence, they set up their banners. But Reader! do not fail at the same time to put down this different conduct to the right cause. Left to themselves in the former instance, we see what human strength is. Aided and encouraged by the Lord's prophets, and more especially the Lord's grace, in this latter instance, we see what man can do, the Lord helping. Precious Jesus! I can do nothing by myself except to sin and forget thee. But I can do all things when thou art by and guidest me on, and enablest me. (Hawker, Poor Man's Old Testament Commentary: 1 Kings-Esther, 603)

Footnote:
1. Proverbs 16:7.

6

Reading: Ezra 6

"Leave the construction of the house of God alone. Let the governor and elders of the Jews rebuild this house of God on its original site. I hereby issue a decree concerning what you are to do, so that the elders of the Jews can rebuild the house of God: The cost is to be paid in full to these men out of the royal revenues ..." Ezra 6:7-8

Observe how the hand of the Lord is with this decree. *Tatnai* and his companions are reproved for opposing God's work. *Darius* not only commands the temple to be built, but at his own cost and charge. Nay more, he makes allowance for the daily sacrifice; and desires that in this temple prayers and sacrifices may be continually offered for the life of himself and his sons. Yea, as if under the spirit of prophecy, he looks up to God to vindicate his own cause in destroying kings as well as people, whosoever shall put forth a hand to the ruin of the temple. Surely one is led almost to believe, that such a friend to God's cause must be a partaker of God's grace. Was not this another instance of the Jew and Gentile being alike interested in Jesus? Solomon's temple had a *Hiram*, king of Tyre, to give aid: and here is a *Darius*, king of Persia, contributing to the second temple. Were not both, blessed Jesus, meant by thee to prefigure the united church of thy glorious redemption, as including both the Jew and the Gentile? (Hawker, Poor Man's Old Testament Commentary: 1 Kings-Esther, 606)

7

Reading: Ezra 7

"... and salt without limit." Ezra 7:22

Salt was used in every offering made by fire unto the Lord, and from its preserving and purifying properties it was the grateful emblem of divine grace in the soul. It is worthy of our attentive regard that, when Artaxerxes gave salt to Ezra the priest, he set no limit to the quantity, and we may be quite certain that when the King of kings distributes grace among his royal priesthood, the supply is not cut short by him. Often are we straitened in ourselves, but never in the Lord. He who chooses to gather much manna will find that he may have as much as he desires. There is no such famine in Jerusalem that the citizens should eat their bread by weight and drink their water by measure. Some things in the economy of grace are measured; for instance our vinegar and gall are given us with such exactness that we never have a single drop too much, but of the salt of grace no stint is made, "Ask what thou wilt and it shall be given unto thee."[1] Parents need to lock up the fruit cupboard, and the sweet jars, but there is no need to keep the salt-box under lock and key, for few children will eat too greedily from that. A man may have too much money, or too much honor, but he cannot have too much grace. When Jeshurun waxed fat in the flesh, he kicked against God,[2] but there is no fear of a man's becoming too full of grace: a plethora of grace is impossible. More wealth brings more care, but more grace brings more joy. Increased wisdom is increased sorrow, but abundance of the Spirit is fulness of joy. Believer, go to the throne for a large supply of heavenly salt. It will season thine afflictions, which are unsavory without salt; it will preserve thy heart which corrupts if salt be absent, and it will kill thy sins even as salt kills reptiles. Thou needest much; seek much, and have much. (Spurgeon, Morning, Dec 13)

Footnotes:
1. Matthew 7:7; Luke 11:9; James 1:5.
2. Deuteronomy 32:15.

8

Reading: Ezra 8

"I did this because I was ashamed to ask the king for infantry and cavalry to protect us from enemies during the journey, since we had told him, "The hand of our God is gracious to all who seek him, but his fierce anger is against all who abandon him." Ezra 8:22

A convoy on many accounts would have been desirable for the pilgrim band, but a holy shame-facedness would not allow Ezra to seek one. He feared lest the heathen king should think his professions of faith in God to be mere hypocrisy, or imagine that the God of Israel was not able to preserve his own worshippers. He could not bring his mind to lean on an arm of flesh in a matter so evidently of the Lord, and therefore the caravan set out with no visible protection, guarded by him who is the sword and shield of his people. It is to be feared that few believers feel this holy jealousy for God; even those who in a measure walk by faith, occasionally mar the luster of their life by craving aid from man. It is a most blessed thing to have no props and no buttresses, but to stand upright on the Rock of Ages, upheld by the Lord alone. Would any believers seek state endowments for their Church, if they remembered that the Lord is dishonored by their asking Caesar's aid? as if the Lord could not supply the needs of his own cause! Should we run so hastily to friends and relations for assistance, if we remembered that the Lord is magnified by our implicit reliance upon his solitary arm? My soul, wait thou only upon God. "But," says one, "are not means to be used?" Assuredly they are; but our fault seldom lies in their neglect: far more frequently it springs out of foolishly believing in them instead of believing in God. Few run too far in neglecting the creature's arm; but very many sin greatly in making too much of it. Learn, dear reader, to glorify the Lord by leaving means untried, if by using them thou wouldst dishonor the name of the Lord. (Spurgeon, Morning, Sep 24)

9

Reading: Ezra 9

Reader! what sweet and gracious signs of sorrow, and of real communion with God. The blushing, and dropping countenance, under the conscious sense of the divine presence, are among the truest tokens of this state of the soul. Reader! do not fail to remark the precious lesson held forth to all true believers in Christ in this example. We as fully enjoy the manifestations of Jesus, and the love of Jehovah in him, when we lie low in the dust before him, as when in those rapturous moments we are like the apostles in the mount of transfiguration, and the Son of God unveils to us his glories, and our interest in him.[1] I stay not to particularize the several features of Ezra's devotion: I rather desire the Reader to mark, in his own view of things, the leading points in it, which bespeak the gracious impressions he was under. The general confession of the sins of Israel he dwells upon, and takes care to point out the part he himself took in them. Every gracious soul doth this, and in his approaches to the mercy-seat feels his own as if they were the heaviest. And how sweetly doth he dwell upon the divine mercies, in their abundance, fulness, and continuance: as if the Lord had taken occasion, from man's undeservings, to magnify his mercy, and the exceeding riches of his grace; that where *sin abounded, grace did much more abound.*[2] Never, blessed Jesus, was there an instance like to thine, when thou camest to seek and save *that which was lost?*[3] I beg the Reader to notice these precious things in Ezra's holy mourning before the throne and mercy-seat. A more beautiful instance of the powerful effects of grace upon the soul, except in the parallel humblings of Daniel, (Chapter 9) is not to be found in the Bible. But I cannot dismiss this view of Ezra, without calling on the Reader to mark one feature more in his approach to God upon this occasion, and the more so because it leads my soul to yet an higher subject, from whence, if I mistake not, the whole virtue and efficacy of Ezra's devotion derived its strength. I mean *the spreading* out his hands unto the Lord his God, meaning God in covenant, as his God in Christ. Doth it not carry the Reader's mind, on the wings of faith, to Calvary, where Jesus' arms were stretched out on the cross, as if in a twofold posture of entreaty, both with God and man. Can we behold Ezra stretching forth his hands in supplication for Israel on this occasion, and shall we forget, or overlook thee, thou blessed Jesus, whose precious feet were fixed to the cross, while thine arms were stretched forth, at once looking up to the Father in intercession, and spread abroad below to embrace all that came to thee, as if saying, *Behold me, behold me; look unto me and be ye saved, all the ends of the earth; for I am God, and there is none else, and beside me there is no Savior.*[4] (Hawker, Poor Man's Old Testament Commentary: 1 Kings-Esther, 622–623)

Footnotes:
1. Matthew 17:4-5.
2. Romans 5:20.
3. Luke 19:10.
4. Isaiah 65:1; 45:21-22.

10

Reading: Ezra 10

Pause, my soul, over this chapter, and before I close this book of divine inspiration, and shut up the view of this great man's history and reform; see, and consider what the Holy Spirit graciously intended to teach the church from it of a spiritual, gospel nature.

And here, my soul, stand still and consider how much of thine own life and conduct is strikingly set forth. Have I not from the womb been seeking out and forming strange alliances, and taking up connection with anything, and with everything, rather than being married to Christ? In Adam and his stock, fallen, sinful, and polluted I was born; by nature closely attached to him, and seeking nothing but what proved my alliance to him. Married to the law, wedded to my own righteousness, (or rather my fancied righteousness, for in reality righteousness I had none); how did I seek to find justification before God by the works of the law? And though that law became only the ministration of death; though its demands of unsinning obedience, making no one allowance whatever, might have made my very soul tremble under its universally condemning power; yet notwithstanding its rigor; notwithstanding the dreadful condemnation it held forth; still infatuated to my own present and everlasting ruin, never should I have put away those strange wives had not Jesus, like another *Ezra*, have come with grace in his lips, and love in his heart, and by his Holy Spirit *convinced me of sin, of righteousness, and of judgment*,[1] and divorcing me from every other alliance, betrothed me to himself, and made me his forever. Oh! thou almighty Bridegroom of thy church and of thy people! what unknown, unexplored riches are contained in that tender character. Yes! my soul! *thy Maker is thine husband, the Lord of Hosts is his name. And thy Redeemer, the God of the whole earth, shall he be called.*[2] Help me, Jesus, my Lord and my God, to put away all the strange alliances my poor sinful heart hath been making. Do thou, dearest Jesus, hedge up my path, my way, with thorns, if at any time my wandering soul should be going away from thee after my old lovers! oh! draw me, thou dear Lord Jesus, that I may run after thee; and be thou my *Ishi*, my husband, my Holy One, the Lord my righteousness. (Hawker, Poor Man's Old Testament Commentary: 1 Kings-Esther, 629)

Footnotes:
1. John 16:7–8.
2. Isaiah 54:5.

11

Reading: Esther 1

"*He held a feast in the third year of his reign for all his officials and staff, the army of Persia and Media, the nobles, and the officials from the provinces. He displayed the glorious wealth of his kingdom and the magnificent splendor of his greatness for a total of 180 days.*" Esther 1:3-4

Who can read the account here given of the royalty and liberality of the Persian monarch, without having the mind immediately directed to look at the Lord Jesus, in his royalty and grace, and to consider both the extent of his bounty, and the honor of his excellent majesty, compared to which this earthly potentate sinks to nothing? What though his kingdom reached over a hundred and seven-and-twenty provinces, from India to Ethiopia; what is this to him, whose dominion is "from sea to sea, and from the river even unto the ends of the earth;" yea, who hath "all power in heaven and in earth," and hath "the keys of hell and the grave?"[1] And what a day, in point of duration, was that feast, which, though extended to a hundred and fourscore, yet, when ended, left nothing to follow, but perhaps induced sickness and sorrow, when we contemplate that eternal and everlasting day, to which Jesus invites, and in which he entertains all his people, whom he hath made "kings and priests unto God and the Father,"[2] and where they shall not only feast with him, and he with them, but shall sit down with him on his throne, as he hath overcome, and is sat down with his Father on his throne?[3] And in this one eternal and never-ending feast of the Lord Jesus, from which the guests shall go out no more, there is nothing to nauseate, nothing unpleasant to mingle, but all is light, and joy, and peace, and unspeakable felicity. Here Jesus openly showeth the riches of his glorious kingdom, and the honor of his excellent majesty! Here he brings his redeemed into a perfect acquaintance with himself, and opens to their astonished, unceasing contemplation and delight the wonders of his person, and the wonders of his love; and fills their ravished souls "with joy unspeakable and full of glory," in the knowledge of "the mystery of God, and of the Father, and of Christ."[4] Hail! thou glorious King of kings, and Lord of lords! Here thou art making a feast of grace in thine holy mountain, for all thy poor and needy, and halt and blind, whom thou hast made the princes of thy kingdom, and whom thou wilt bring, in thine own good time, to the everlasting feast of glory in thy kingdom above! Grant me, blessed Jesus, to be one of the happy number who partake of thy bounties of grace here, and, sure I am, that I shall then one day sit down to the everlasting enjoyment of thyself in the glories of heaven forever! (Hawker, The Poor Man's Evening Portion, Sep 21)

Footnotes:
1. Psalm 72:8; Matthew 28:18; Revelation 1:18.
2. Revelation 1:6; 5:10.
3. Hebrews 10:12.
4. 1 Peter 1:8; Colossians 2:2.

12

Reading: Esther 2

"*When Mordecai learned of the plot, he reported it to Queen Esther, and she told the king on Mordecai's behalf.*" Esther 2:22

I request the Reader not to lose sight of this transaction, particularly the part that Mordecai had in it; for it became a point of great importance in the sequel of Mordecai's life. This small event, as it should seem to have been respecting Mordecai, the Lord graciously overruled, when a deep and desperate attempt was made against the church in the after stages of cruelty intended to be exercised upon it, and by it accomplished the church's deliverance. By small means sometimes the Lord carrieth on the secret purposes of his holy will. It is beautiful to mark how the Lord doth this in all our own concerns. The Psalmist saith, that *whoso is wise will ponder these things, they shall understand the loving kindness of the Lord.*[1] (Hawker, Poor Man's Old Testament Commentary: 1 Kings-Esther, 701)

Footnote:
1. Psalm 107:43.

13

Reading: Esther 3

"... But Mordecai would not bow down or pay homage." Esther 3:2

At the first reading of this passage, it may seem somewhat extraordinary to a common Reader, that Mordecai should refuse to pay homage to Haman. But the reason will soon be discovered, when we call to mind what God had commanded his people on this point. Haman, we are told, was an Agagite; a descendant, therefore, of that Agag, who was king of the Amalekites; against whom the Lord had sworn, that his people should have *war, from generation to generation*. Hence, therefore, Mordecai considered the Lord's command, and refused to bow down to an Amalekite: so that nothing can be more beautiful in proof of Mordecai's faithfulness. Though his life was at stake, and he knew that the absolute power of the king might order him to death without trial; yet he feared not the wrath of the king, like another champion for the truth of old, for *he endured, as seeing him who is invisible*.[1] (Hawker, Poor Man's Old Testament Commentary: 1 Kings-Esther, 703)

Footnote:
1. Exodus 17:14–16; Deuteronomy 25:17–19; 1 Samuel 15:2-3, 32-33; Hebrews 11:7.

14

Reading: Esther 4

"Go and assemble all the Jews who can be found in Susa and fast for me. Don't eat or drink for three days, night or day. I and my female servants will also fast in the same way." Esther 4:16

How the Lord wrought upon the mind of Esther is evident from what is here said. She enters not upon the service to which she was called, without first looking up to the Lord both for a blessing and direction. Reader! she did as I pray God you and I may have the same grace to do upon all undertakings for God's glory, and our own happiness; she sought to God according to that blessed promise, which thousands have found true, and none ever failed in: In *all thy ways acknowledge him, and he will direct thy paths.*[1] And it is a maxim sooner or later to be depended upon, he that begins in prayer will find cause to end in praise. I admire the piety of Esther. She was indeed a true Israelite in setting up a fast herself, and in calling upon the church to the same. Here was a sweet example of what is frequently spoken of, but not so generally regarded, the communion of Saints. Though Esther and the Jews of the city of *Shushan*, were separated by walls and absent in body, yet were they present in Spirit. And oh! what might we not expect to follow such spiritual converse among the people of God, when we call to mind that one and the same Almighty Spirit, is the quickener of all, the helper of the infirmities of all, and maketh *intercession for the saints according to the will of God.*² The resolution Esther took of going in uncalled before the king, was highly proper and noble. God in covenant is a sure God; and in all cases which are for his glory and his people's welfare, he will manifest himself their helper. But (as if Esther had said) if there be a doubt concerning this particular providence now pending, if the Lord hath given us up to chastisement, I can but perish; and if I do, I will yet die trusting. Reader! while we admire this woman's faith, let you and I seek grace to exercise that faith yet higher. None can perish who hang on God's covenant engagements in Jesus. And therefore, to say (as some do say,) if I perish, I will perish at Christ's feet, is a contradiction in itself, and plainly manifests that their faith who say so, is not what it should be. Oh! for faith to believe the record which God hath given of his Son. And in this faith to go in before the king of Kings, and lord of Lords, with a firmness of assurance like Job. *Will he plead against me* (saith Job) *with his great power? No. But he will put strength in me. There the righteous might dispute with him; so shall I be delivered forever from my judge.*³ Reader! pause, and admire the grace of faith given to this man. And while you admire, beg of God to be made a partaker of the same. Surely, the true believing soul in Jesus, if he gives credit to the word of Jehovah, or the infinitely precious value of the Redeemer's blood and righteousness, can never fear to perish, while secured in the double stronghold of God the Father's sovereign grace, and God the Son's justifying righteousness. Lord! grant in this faith my soul may daily, hourly live, and in this perfect assurance die. Amen. (Hawker, Poor Man's Old Testament Commentary: 1 Kings-Esther, 710)

Footnotes:
1. Proverbs 3:6.
2. Romans 8:26-27.
3. Job 23:6-7.

15

Reading: Esther 5

"And the king said unto Esther at the banquet of wine, 'What is thy petition? and it shall be granted thee: And what is thy request? even to the half of the kingdom it shall be performed.'" Esther 5:6 (AKJV)

My soul! thou hast lately been at the banquet of wine indeed, even of the Redeemer's blood, which Jesus holds at his table; and didst thou not behold the numberless petitioners who attended there with thyself? Surely, if the Persian king made so generous an offer to Esther, to perform her petition, be it what it might, to the half of his kingdom, thy Jesus, thy heavenly King, with whom are all the treasures, and the unsearchable riches of grace and glory,[1] did not suffer a poor humble petitioner to go empty away. Tell me, ye that attended there, did ye not find the King most gracious? How went the matter with you? I pray you tell me. Did the poor man find Jesus indeed rich; and did the trembling sinner, under the apprehension of wrath, find himself delivered by him "from the wrath to come?"[2] Surely, Jesus had a suited mercy for every case. And, sure I am, that the heart that was prompted by his grace to look to him, the eye and heart of Jesus, were looking with mercy upon that poor sinner. Oh! what gifts, what graces, what pardons, doth every renewed banquet of Jesus scatter among the people! At his table the doors are thrown open, and nothing is needed to ensure welcome, but a sense of need and a hungering to partake. How often, my soul, hast thou seen the people made joyful in the Lord's house of prayer, and returning, as they did after the feast of the dedication of Solomon's temple, to their tents, "joyful and glad in heart?" Yea, how often hast thou returned thyself, and left all thy sorrows, sins, and wants behind thee, when the King hath held forth his scepter of grace, and given thee faith to touch it! Come, ye polluted, poor, exercised, distressed souls, ye wandering, weary, backsliding people; come to Jesus; he holds a feast, and every case and every need, he can, and will supply. Let but a sense of need be inwrought by the blessed Spirit in the heart, and the language of our Jesus is to this amount: "What is thy petition, and what is thy request? and it shall be granted thee." (Hawker, The Poor Man's Evening Portion, Oct 11)

Footnotes:
1. Colossians 2:2-4; Ephesians 3:7-9.
2. 1 Thessalonians 1:10.

16

Reading: Esther 6

"What shall be done to the man whom the king delighteth to honor?"
Esther 6:6 (AKJV)

    Nay, my soul, ask thine own heart what shall be done to the God-man whom Jehovah, the King of kings, delighteth to honor? Oh! for the view of what John saw, and to hear what John heard, when he beheld heaven opened, and heard the innumerable multitude chanting Salvation to God and the Lamb![1] Lord, I would say, let every knee bow before him, and every tongue confess that Jesus Christ is Lord, to the glory of God the Father.[2] And oh! most gracious Father, dost thou take delight that Jesus should be honored? Is it thine honor when Jesus is honored; thy glory when Jesus is glorified? Oh! what wonderful encouragement is this to the faith and belief of a poor sinner; that I not only praise my adorable Redeemer when I come to him for all things, and trust him for all things; but these exercises of grace are as acceptable to God my Father, as they are honorable to God the Son. And this is the only way, and a blessed way it is indeed, by which a poor sinner can give glory to the Father, in believing the record which he hath given of his

Son. Here, then, my soul, do thou daily be found in honoring the Glory-man, the God-man Christ Jesus, whom God the Father delighteth to honor. (Hawker, The Poor Man's Morning Portion, Jan 20)

Footnotes:
1. Revelation 7:9-11.
2. Philippians 2:9-11.

17

Reading: Esther 7

Reader! do not let the history of this wretched man Haman pass away from thy mind, without leaving the suitable reflections the review of such an awful character ought to occasion. What our blessed Lord said of some in his days seems applicable to some in all the days of the Church; *Ye are* (said Jesus to them) *of your father the devil, and the lusts of your father ye will do; he was a murderer from the beginning.*[1] And what a resemblance doth the character of Haman bear to such a stock? His hatred to poor Mordecai, stirred up by the evil spirit, disdained to shew itself against an individual only; the whole race shall die. Inflamed by power, by pride, and a troop of evil passions, he prosecutes his implacable malice, and to the attainment of this one object he would sacrifice every other. Pause, Reader, as you contemplate the man. Recollect that the same depravity is every man's by nature; and, but for grace, the evil which one man feels disposed to do, all would feel disposed to do. Nothing makes the difference, but the sovereign, free, restraining, preventing, and renewing grace of God in Jesus. Oh! for a thorough sense of this upon the heart! Oh! for a more awakened knowledge of our infinite and eternal mercies in Jesus. Oh! forever blessed, blessed be God for Jesus Christ.

One word more before we quit this chapter. See, Reader, in Esther's suit obtained, after all the difficulties which seemed to lay in the way, that the cause of God's people can never be overlooked, nor forgotten. Hence, then, let us gather a renewed evidence that in Jesus and his great salvation are everlastingly secured to his people all the blessings contained in redemption. Trials, and difficulties, and seemingly impossibilities of deliverance, may, and must indeed, beset the people of Jesus in their way: but never forget this; Jesus is everlastingly pursuing one invariable plan of happiness concerning them. Oh! for grace to love Jesus, and to know Jesus as a friend, even when in his providences he seems to frown as though he was an enemy. Oh! for grace to lean upon one arm, when with the other he is correcting; to cleave to him, when we cannot take comfort from the darkness of his ways towards us. By and by (the soul saith) he will appear to my joy: I shall behold his face in righteousness. I know that all the ways of the Lord are mercy and truth. Things are now dark; but the morning will come. Oh! for grace, then, to wait the Lord's time, and to be convinced that all things must and do work together for good to them that love God, and are the called according to his purpose. (Hawker, Poor Man's Old Testament Commentary: 1 Kings-Esther, 721–722)

Footnote:
1. John 8:44.

18

Reading: Esther 8

Of all the sweet reflections which arise out of this chapter, (and many and interesting they are), I desire chiefly to have my soul directed to the contemplation of Jesus, in his love to this people which the anxiety of Esther, for her countrymen the Jews, so strongly prompts the mind to consider. If she felt such concern as to cry out, 'How can I endure to see the evil that shall come unto my people; or how can I endure to see the destruction of my kindred?' Think, Reader, whether it be possible to conceive Jesus will look on, and suffer any of his to perish? Recollect the interest he hath in them, the relationship in which he stands towards them; the purchase he hath made of them; the vast price they cost him; the love he hath to his Father who gave them to him; and the pains he hath gone through, to make their salvation sure? And can you suppose it possible, that he will suffer one of those little ones, which trust in him, to perish? Consider what he is in himself: His glory, greatness, almightiness, and sovereignty, as God and man in one person. Consider what he is in his alliance with his people: There is not a relationship in nature but Jesus fills. He is our everlasting Father. *As one whom his Father comforteth,* (he saith himself) *so will I comfort you.*[1] He is the husband of his church, the brother, the friend. In short, under the tenderest and most endearing characters, he condescends to represent himself, as if by way of confirming his love, which is stronger than death and more vehement in its warmth than coals of fire. And consider what Jesus hath done to satisfy their souls, in the assurance of his unalterable love. He assumed the very nature of man, to convince man by such a palpable evidence of it, how his heart was towards his people. And having stood up as our surety, borne our sins, carried our sorrows, and though knowing no sin in himself, yet being made sin, and even a curse for us, and having satisfied the divine justice, answered the whole law, taken the punishment, finished transgression, made an end of sin, brought in an everlasting righteousness, washed poor sinners in his blood, clothed them in his righteousness, he now ever liveth to see the whole purposes of his salvation, fully accomplished: can He endure to see any evil upon his people; or those for whom he died brought into everlasting ruin? Can Jesus look on and behold the destruction of his kindred? Reader! think of this and cast thy soul upon him who careth for thee? Oh! precious Jesus! I would say, cause me to rest with full assurance of faith, and to triumph in thee and thy great salvation! (Hawker, Poor Man's Old Testament Commentary: 1 Kings-Esther, 726–727)

Footnote:
1. 2 Corinthians 1:3-4.

19

Reading: Esther 9

My soul! while proclamations are made and religiously observed, for the annual celebration of deliverances; do thou get away to the mountain of holiness, in the gospel Church of Jesus, and daily celebrate that great deliverance from the wrath to come, which the Son of God by his glorious undertaking and accomplishment, wrought out for poor sinners, who are brought to believe in his name. Here is an everlasting festival indeed, opened to thy unceasing contemplation and thy joy. And here it is that we find *the kingdom of God not meat and drink, but righteousness, and peace, and joy in the Holy Spirit.*[1] Here then, my soul, seek grace from God, to celebrate in a constant jubilee, thy deliverance from the curse of God's law, the alarms of thine own conscience, the terrors of a guilty mind, with all the just apprehensions of the wrath to come. Blessed be God! the king's decree hath been published and sent through all the provinces: Jesus gives grace, mercy, and peace. And *God so loved the world, that he sent his only begotten Son, to the end that all that believe in him should not perish, but have everlasting life.*[2] And God the Holy

Spirit confirms the glorious truth, in giving poor sinners grace *to believe the record which God hath given of his Son.* Lord! cause my soul to receive the truth in the love of it: and oh! grant that I may by faith live in the daily enjoyment of it; and at length arrive to the everlasting celebration of it in the realms above, where Jesus will be eternally adored, and praises of redemption be unceasingly offered to *God and the Lamb.* (Hawker, Poor Man's Old Testament Commentary: 1 Kings-Esther, 731–732)

Footnotes:
1. Romans 14:17.
2. John 3:16.

20

Reading: Esther 10

"... He continued to pursue prosperity for his people ..." Esther 10:3

Mordecai was a true patriot, and therefore, being exalted to the highest position under Ahasuerus, he used his eminence to promote the prosperity of Israel. In this he was a type of Jesus, who, upon his throne of glory, seeks not his own, but spends his power for his people. It were well if every Christian would be a Mordecai to the church, striving according to his ability for its prosperity. Some are placed in stations of affluence and influence, let them honor their Lord in the high places of the earth, and testify for Jesus before great men. Others have what is far better, namely, close fellowship with the King of kings, let them be sure to plead daily for the weak of the Lord's people, the doubting, the tempted, and the comfortless. It will redound to their honor if they make much intercession for those who are in darkness and dare not draw nigh unto the mercy seat. Instructed believers may serve their Master greatly if they lay out their talents for the general good, and impart their wealth of heavenly learning to others, by teaching them the things of God. The very least in our Israel may at least seek the welfare of his people; and his desire, if he can give no more, shall be acceptable. It is at once the most Christlike and the most happy course for a believer to cease from living to himself. He who blesses others cannot fail to be blessed himself. On the other hand, to seek our own personal greatness is a wicked and unhappy plan of life, its way will be grievous, and its end will be fatal.

Here is the place to ask thee, my friend, whether thou art to the best of thy power seeking the wealth of the church in thy neighborhood? I trust thou art not doing it mischief by bitterness and scandal, nor weakening it by thy neglect. Friend, unite with the Lord's poor, bear their cross, do them all the good thou canst, and thou shalt not miss thy reward. (Spurgeon, Eve, Nov 28)

21

Reading: Nehemiah 1

How truly lovely doth Nehemiah appear in the account here given of him. Not all the splendor of a court, nor the favor of a king, could make him forget the interests of his own country, or prevent tears from running down when he considered the affliction of Zion. Think of this, my soul, in the best moments of any outward providences, and take part in the concerns of the church of Jesus. Doth the church of Jesus lay waste? Are the dear members of his mystical body in affliction? Do they hunger while thou art full? Are they oppressed, and thou takest no part in their oppression? Oh! how canst thou be counted part of Jesus. Oh! gracious God and Savior, grant to me such a sympathizing spirit in all that concerns thy cause and interest in the earth, that I may never, never lose sight of the wonderful price thy church cost thee, when for redemption thou didst shed thy precious blood. Animate, my soul, I beseech thee, thou Holy Spirit of grace, with the same fire from thine holy altar, as thou didst thy servant the prophet, that like him I may besiege the mercy-seat with clamorous and unceasing petitions, resolving, for *Zion's sake, never to hold my peace, and for Jerusalem's sake never to rest, until the righteousness thereof go forth as brightness, and the salvation thereof as a lamp that burneth.*[1]

Behold, my soul also, in this sweet chapter, the mighty privilege of a throne of grace. Behold in this instance of Nehemiah, that no place, no clime, no country, no situation, is in itself able to keep the awakened soul from God. That throne which John saw surrounded with a rainbow is accessible on every side. Jesus, the Lamb, is in the midst of it. He still hears prayers; still feeds the church which he hath purchased with his blood; still acts as a priest upon his throne; wears thy nature and the priesthood still; and is infinitely more ready to take in petitions and bestow blessings than his people are to ask or receive. Oh! Lord Jesus! I would say, hear me then for myself, for my country, for thy church, for thy people! *do good in thy good pleasure unto Zion; build up her walls and love her still.* (Hawker, Poor Man's Old Testament Commentary: 1 Kings-Esther, 633–634)

Footnote:
1. Isaiah 62:1.

22

Reading: Nehemiah 2

Mark, my soul, the very different characters which distinguish men of the world from real lovers of God. Their features, manners, customs, pursuits, habits, pleasures, all differ. Whatever root of bitterness it is, I do not presume to say, but certain it is that there is a root of bitterness springing up within them, both the blossom and the baleful deadly fruit appear in all their branches. But while these marks plainly testify whose they are, and in whose cause they are planted; how blessed is it to see that they can extend their luxuriancy no farther than the Lord allows. And how further blessed it is to see, that the Lord makes use of them medicinally to his people for good. *Sanballat* and *Tobiah* meant not so, neither did their heart intend it; but yet, in reality, all they did, and all their scoffs and oppositions, only tended to make Nehemiah more assiduous, and more earnest in his recourses to a mercy seat. Reader! when our enemies do this; when they drive us to a throne of grace, when otherwise we should not go there, surely the Lord by his overruling wisdom converts their very evil into good, and compels them, contrary to their wishes and intent, to prove our kind friends.

Mark, my soul, in *Nehemiah*, the portrait of God's children. While the Lord's house lies waste, they take no pleasure. While Jesus and his people are oppressed, there is no joy in a gracious soul. See then, my soul, whether, like Nehemiah, thou art anxious for the prosperity of Zion? Can a throne of grace witness for thee, that thy petitions are lodged there for her welfare? Dost thou love her courts, her ordinances, her servants, her ministers, her people? Is the Lord himself precious to thee, and dearer than the golden wedge of Ophir? Oh! thou dear Redeemer! let thy name, thy person, thy work, thine offices, thy character, relations; all, all that belongs to Jesus, be as ointment poured forth. And oh! grant, my Lord, that I may be a sweet savor of Jesus, as Nehemiah, to all around. (Hawker, Poor Man's Old Testament Commentary: 1 Kings-Esther, 638)

23

Reading: Nehemiah 3

"The king's garden." Nehemiah 3:15

Mention of the king's garden by Nehemiah brings to mind the paradise which the King of kings prepared for Adam. Sin has utterly ruined that fair abode of all delights, and driven forth the children of men to till the ground, which yields thorns and briers unto them. My soul, remember the fall, for it was *thy* fall. Weep much because the Lord of love was so shamefully ill-treated by the head of the human race, of which thou art a member, as undeserving as any. Behold how dragons and demons dwell on this fair earth, which once was a garden of delights.

See yonder another King's garden, which the King waters with his bloody sweat – *Gethsemane*, whose bitter herbs are sweeter far to renewed souls than even Eden's luscious fruits. There the mischief of the serpent in the first garden was undone: there the curse was lifted from earth, and borne by the woman's promised seed. My soul, bethink thee much of the agony and the passion; resort to the garden of the olive-press, and view thy great Redeemer rescuing thee from thy lost estate. This is the garden of gardens indeed, wherein the soul may see the guilt of sin and the power of love, two sights which surpass all others.

Is there no other King's garden? Yes, *my heart*, thou art, or shouldst be such. How do the flowers flourish? Do any choice fruits appear? Does the King walk within, and rest in the bowers of my spirit? Let me see that the plants are trimmed and watered, and the mischievous foxes hunted out. Come, Lord, and let the heavenly wind blow at thy coming, that the spices of thy garden may flow abroad. Nor must I forget the King's garden of *the church*. O Lord, send prosperity unto it. Rebuild her walls, nourish her plants, ripen her fruits, and from the huge wilderness, reclaim the barren waste, and make thereof "a King's garden." (Spurgeon, Eve, Apr 12)

24

Reading: Nehemiah 4

"From that day on, half of my men did the work while the other half held spears, shields, bows, and armor." Nehemiah 4:16

I hope the Reader will again and again, as he passeth through this whole chapter, carry his thoughts beyond the literal relation, to the contemplation of the church of God as represented in it. The Christian is both a warrior, and a builder: and sure he is, in every stage of his pursuit, in building the temple of the Lord, to meet with opposition. In all ages there have been *Sanballats* and *Tobiahs*. Like Nehemiah's servants, God's people must have the sword of the Spirit to oppose the adversary; and the whole armor of salvation, *on the right hand, and on the left*. It is on this account the apostle admonisheth the Ephesian Church *to be strong in the Lord, and in the power of his might*.[1] (Hawker, Poor Man's Old Testament Commentary: 1 Kings-Esther, 646)

Footnote:
1. Ephesians 6:10-20.

25

Reading: Nehemiah 5

"Furthermore, from the day King Artaxerxes appointed me to be their governor in the land of Judah ... I and my associates never ate from the food allotted to the governor ... Instead, I devoted myself to the construction of this wall, and all my subordinates were gathered there for the work. We didn't buy any land." Nehemiah 5:14-16

There is much to admire in this liberality of Nehemiah, who would not avail himself of his office, as governor under the king of Persia his master, to take money or goods from the people. He lost sight of his authority in this particular, in his affection as a Jew. He considered himself as a brother, and as such acted the brotherly part. He must have been a noble character. But oh! at what an infinite distance doth Nehemiah stand, in this nobleness of soul, when we look at the Lord Jesus Christ. He who was rich, yet *for our sakes became poor, that we through his poverty might be made rich*.[1] It was generous for Nehemiah to leave the court of Persia to visit Jerusalem in ruins. But what was this, in point of greatness of love, compared to thine, thou adorable, blessed Jesus, in that thou didst leave the court of heaven, and the bosom of thy Father, and camest not *to be ministered unto, but to minister, and to give thy life a ransom for many?*[2] Oh! matchless love! Oh! unequalled, unheard-of grace! (Hawker, Poor Man's Old Testament Commentary: 1 Kings-Esther, 650)

Footnotes:
1. 2 Corinthians 8:9.
2. Matthew 20:28; Mark 10:45.

26

Reading: Nehemiah 6

"I am doing a great work, so that I cannot come down: why should the work cease, whilst I leave it and come down to you?" Nehemiah 6:3 (AKJV)

My soul! a very blessed instruction is held forth to thee, in these words. *Nehemiah* met with sad interruptions in his service, while building the Lord's house. Various were the attempts made by the enemies of God and his cause, to call him off from his labors. But this was his answer to all. Now, my soul, thou hast many enemies also, both from within and without; the world, and the powers of darkness, and thine own corruptions, are all in league to interrupt thy pursuit of divine things. When, therefore, the *Sanballats* and the *Geshems* of the day invite thee to the villages, in the plain of *Ono*, here is thine answer: "Why should the work of the Lord cease, when the King's business requires dispatch?" Wherefore should the body, with all its corrupt affections, drag down the soul? Is it reasonable, is it proper to be concerned for the things of a day, while regardless of eternity? Wilt thou forever be as little children amused with toys, and taken up with playthings, when Jesus is calling thee, and proposing himself to thee, for thy constant, unceasing, present, and everlasting delight? Oh! for grace and strength from the Lord, to be able, like Abraham, to fray away those fowls which come down upon the sacrifice! O do thou, Lord, drive both the buyers and the sellers from thy temple![1] Take my whole heart and soul, and all my affections, and fix and center them all on thyself! Every vanity, every robber, like *Barabbas* of old, will be preferred to thee, thou dear Emmanuel, unless thy grace restrain and keep under what thy grace hath taught me to know and feel, that I carry about with me a body of sin and death, which is forever calling me aside from thee. Oh! let thy grace make its way through all the swarms of vain thoughts and interruptions which surround me, and make my soul "as the chariots of Amminadib!" Let no longer these "dead flies spoil the excellent ointment," made fragrant by the rich spices of thy blessed Spirit: but when even by the most innocent calls, like that made to Jesus himself, of his mother and his brethren being without, desiring to speak to him, oh! for grace, that, like my Lord, even then, I may not suffer the higher claims of my God and Savior to pass by, nor the work of the Lord and the concern of my soul to cease, to come down to them. (Hawker, The Poor Man's Evening Portion, Oct 13)

Footnote:
1. Mark 11:15-16.

27

Reading: Nehemiah 7

"The city was large and spacious, but there were few people in it, and no houses had been built yet." Nehemiah 7:4

It is to be supposed that the holy city of Jerusalem, stood upon the very same ground as before its desolation. And though at present not peopled as heretofore with a multitude of inhabitants, yet looking for the accomplishment of God's promises, the same room as before was taken in.[1] By the appointment of Hanani and Hananiah to the government, it seems probable that Nehemiah was looking forward to his return to the court of Persia. This is the same Hanani which brought tidings to Nehemiah concerning Jerusalem, as mentioned in the first chapter, verse 2. The faithfulness of his partner Hananiah is honorably mentioned. May we not spiritualize the passage in reference to the faithful ministers of Christ, and remark, that if the security of Jerusalem, in its frontiers and gates, became so important, how much more should those who stand at the doors of the Lord's heritage use vigilance and circumspection, to see who are admitted, and that they are indeed of the *true household of faith*.

"These are the people of the province who went up among the captive exiles deported by King Nebuchadnezzar of Babylon. Each of them returned to Jerusalem and Judah, to his own town." Nehemiah 7:6

Here is a register exactly corresponding to the one made in the days of Ezra, though this must have been at least 40 years after.[2] When I say exactly, I mean in all the great and leading points in which the value and faithfulness of the record is made to depend. Though I think it not necessary to detain the Reader with making the same observations upon it which I did on that chapter, yet I cannot help observing that as the Holy Spirit hath thought proper to have this register faithfully handed down to the church both by Ezra and Nehemiah, it may serve to shew us its great importance. And next to the one grand cause of all records of families among God's people, which is wholly with an eye to Jesus, it is not, I think, a subject of small moment to consider also how sweetly it testifies of the love of God the Holy Spirit to the people of Jesus, in that the genealogy is thus twice put down. As if to teach every poor, despised and humble follower of the Lord Jesus, that how little so ever esteemed he may be among men, yet is he of great price in the sight of God. Think of it, my brother, I beseech you. The Reader will not fail to remark also, as a further confirmation of this subject, that Nehemiah expressly saith *the thing was from the Lord. My God* (said he) *put it into my heart.*[3] Oh! how sweet is it to trace all gracious dispositions up to their source!

...The liberal gifts of the people plainly testify their sense of the Lord's presence, and his blessing upon them. In all ages these testimonies are among the truest tokens of the real work of grace upon the heart. (Hawker, Poor Man's Old Testament Commentary: 1 Kings-Esther, 655, 660–661)

Footnotes:
1. Zechariah 7:4–7; 8:3, 6.
2. Ezra 2.
3. Nehemiah 7:5.

28

Reading: Nehemiah 8

"On the second day, the family heads of all the people, along with the priests and Levites, assembled before the scribe Ezra to study the words of the law." Nehemiah 8:13

How blessed is it to follow up the sabbath day's employment in the study of God's word with the next day's attention, bringing to remembrance what we then heard? When the parlor or the kitchen, or those who have neither, make the chamber an echo to the sanctuary, and rehearse among their household, or their friends, or acquaintance, what they heard on the preceding sabbath concerning Jesus. And what encouragement is there to this in God's blessed word! The prophets tells us that *they that feared the name of the Lord were often talking one to another; and the Lord hearkened and heard it.* And the Evangelist tells us that while the disciples of Jesus were talking of him by the way, *Jesus himself drew near and went with them.*[1] Reader! depend upon it, when Jesus, in the sweetness and preciousness of his name, is in the mouth and upon the lips, from the abundance of the heart awakened by grace, the Lord will bless such edifying conversation, and impart greater degrees of knowledge both to speaker and hearer.[2] (Hawker, Poor Man's Old Testament Commentary: 1 Kings-Esther, 664)

Footnotes:
1. Luke 24:15.
2. See Malachi 3:16-17; Luke 24:14-15.

29

Reading: Nehemiah 9

"You are righteous concerning all that has happened to us, because you have acted faithfully, while we have acted wickedly." Nehemiah 9:33

It would be incorrect to suppose that the chastisements of our heavenly Father were in themselves pleasant and desirable. They are no more so than the physician's recipe, or the surgeon's lancet. But as in the one case, so in the other, we look beyond the medicine to its sanative qualities, we forget the bitterness of the draught in its remedial results. Thus, with the medicine of the soul – the afflictions sent and sanctified by God. Forgetting the bitter and the pain of God's dealings, the only question of moment is what the cause is and what the design of my Father in this? The answer is – our deeper sanctification.

This is effected, first, by making us more thoroughly acquainted with the holiness of God Himself. Sanctified chastisement has an especial tendency to this. To suppose a case. Our sense of God's holiness, previously to this dispensation, was essentially defective, unsound, superficial, and uninfluential. The judgment admitted the truth; we could speak of it to others, and in prayer acknowledge it to

God; but still there was vagueness and indistinctness in our conceptions of it, which left the heart cold, and rendered the walk uneven. To be led now into the actual, heart-felt experience of the truth, that in all our transactions we had to deal with the holy, heart-searching Lord God, we find quite another and an advanced stage in our journey, another and a deeper lesson learned in our school. This was the truth, and in this way, Nehemiah was taught. "Howbeit you are just (holy) in all that is brought upon us; for you have done right, but we have done wickedly." Oh, blessed acknowledgment! Do not think that we speak unfeelingly when we say, it was worth all the discipline you have ever passed through, to a have become more deeply schooled in the lesson of God's holiness. One most fruitful cause of all our declensions from the Lord will be found wrapped up in the crude and superficial views which we entertain of the character of God, as a God of infinite purity. And this truth He will have His people to study and to learn, not by sermons, nor from books, not from hearsay, nor from theory, but in the school of loving chastisement – personally and Experimentally [experientially]. Thus, beholding more closely, and through a clearer medium, this Divine perfection, the believer is changed more perfectly into the same moral image. "He for our profit, that we might be partakers of His holiness."[1]

The rod of the covenant has a wonderful power of discovery. Thus, by revealing to us the concealed evil of our natures, we become more holy. "The blueness (that is, the severity) of a wound cleanses away evil."[2] This painful discovery often recalls to memory past failings and sins. David went many years in oblivion of his departure from God, until Nathan was sent, who, while he told him of his sin, with the same breath announced the message of Divine forgiveness.[3] Then it was the royal penitent kneeled down and poured forth from the depths of his anguished spirit the fifty-first Psalm – a portion of God's word which you cannot too frequently study. "I do remember my sin this day," is the exclamation of the chastened sufferer. Thus, led to search into the cause of the Divine correction, and discovering it – perhaps after a long season of forgetfulness – the "blueness of the wound," the severity of the rod, "cleanses away the evil;" in other words, more deeply sanctifies the soul. "Show me why you contend with me." (Winslow, Evening Thoughts, Jun 1)

Footnotes:
1. Hebrews 12:10.
2. Proverbs 20:30.
3. 2 Samuel 12.

30

Reading: Nehemiah 10

"Those whose seals were on the document were the governor Nehemiah ..." Nehemiah 10:1

I did not think it necessary to interrupt the progress of the reading in going over the catalogue of those that signed the covenant. It was not done by all the people, but by the elders and leading men, beginning with the *Tirshatha*, that is the governor; then followed the priests; next to them the Levites; and then the chief of the people; making in all eighty-four persons, including Nehemiah the governor. And we are told that the rest of the people joined in the covenant, both men and their wives, their sons and their daughters; all, as many as were arrived to years of discretion and knowledge. Was not this a type of the gospel church, concerning which the Lord promised in the last days to pour out of his Spirit, that our young men should prophecy, and our old men see visions, and upon the Lord's servants and handmaidens that grace should be given? What a precious thing it is to behold and trace the uniformity between the Jewish and the gospel church; and to discover that the covenant is one and the same being founded in the everlasting love of Jehovah, and summed up and finished in the person and work of the Lord Jesus Christ.

...Here are some of the particulars to which the people pledged themselves by this covenant to be bound. But what I would desire the Reader to regard, as in my esteem being beautifully descriptive of the great feature of the gospel, is the redemption of the first-born of their sons, so strikingly set forth in the law: Exodus 13:11–16. And as this was expressly appointed as typical of the people's deliverance from the bondage of Egypt, nothing can be more plain than that the deliverance from the bondage of sin and death, which that event prefigured, immediately pointed to the person and work of the Lord Jesus Christ. Thus we find in all ages, and in all periods of the church, God the Holy Spirit kept alive in the minds of his people the glorious redemption of the Lord Jesus Christ. And the whole covenant from beginning to end referred to this, and in this had its completion. (Hawker, Poor Man's Old Testament Commentary: 1 Kings-Esther, 673–675)

31

Reading: Nehemiah 11

"The people blessed all the men who volunteered to live in Jerusalem." Nehemiah 11:2

It doth not appear what was the cause that the generality of the people were averse to live in Jerusalem. (As it was the holy city, one might have expected that they would have been more eager to have fixed their residence there, than in the distant villages or lesser towns of Israel). Probably the fear of the enemies of Israel, or the apprehension of the Persian power, under which they were in tribute. Certain it is, however, that those who volunteered to live there were considered true patriots and had the blessing of the people. Reader! even now it requires much grace to step forward in the cause of Jesus, and declare ourselves to be volunteers in his cause. (Hawker, Poor Man's Old Testament Commentary: 1 Kings-Esther, 676)

32

Reading: Nehemiah 12

"The second thanksgiving procession went to the left, and I followed it with half the people along the top of the wall..." Nehemiah 12:38

Nehemiah had very largely described, in the former part of his book, the labors in building the wall; and therefore he will not pass over the dedication of it. The account is truly interesting. And as he himself, though governor, took an active part in the service, it is no wonder that all ranks and orders of the people joined in the festivity. The joy was so great, that their voices and musical instruments were heard afar off. But Reader! think what joy of soul that will be, when *the Lord shall build up Zion, and her glory shall appear.* When the king of Zion shall arise to turn away ungodliness from Jacob! In the longing expectation of this great event, how hath the mind of the faithful been directed in all ages! How fervent the cry which hath in different periods burst from innumerable hearts; Lord, cut short thy work in righteousness, and hasten thy kingdom! (Hawker, Poor Man's Old Testament Commentary: 1 Kings-Esther, 684)

33

Reading: Nehemiah 13

"*While all this was happening, I was not in Jerusalem, because I had returned to King Artaxerxes of Babylon in the thirty-second year of his reign. It was only later that I asked the king for a leave of absence so I could return to Jerusalem...*" Nehemiah 13:6-7

It should seem very plainly from what is here said, that Nehemiah had returned to Persia, and now was come back to Jerusalem. During his absence *Eliashib* the High Priest, to his everlasting disgrace, from his alliance with *Tobiah*, had not only paid this open enemy of God and his church great respect, but had dared to desecrate the temple by giving him an apartment in it: and to make room for him had removed the things belonging to the temple service. What an awful character must have been this High Priest! Oh! how unlike thee, thou great High Priest of our God and of thy people! But stop, my soul; doth not every minister do the same, nay, if possible, worse than *Eliashib*, who substitutes falsehood for truth in the services of the sanctuary? Who teaches the people to accommodate *Tobiahs* of every description and character, instead of Christ?

Alas! alas! what rubbish of anything, of nothing, of worse than nothing, is sometimes made to supply the place of Jesus, and his one-salvation, for poor perishing sinners. Oh! for the spirit given to Nehemiah to reform these abuses, to be poured out now, that an holy zeal might cast forth the false refuges of lies out of the Lord's chambers wherever they are found. (Hawker, Poor Man's Old Testament Commentary: 1 Kings-Esther, 687)

34

Reading: Psalm 126

Reader! in the perusal of this Psalm, I would beg of you, as I desire to examine myself, to look and see whether we really bear a part in the triumphs here recorded. The effects of this deliverance are very strikingly defined; the joy of the soul was such, that from its greatness it seemed but as a dream. Such is the real joy when Christ converts, and brings the sinner from the captivity of sin and Satan. Convinced of sin, and converted by the Holy Spirit to the belief of salvation by Jesus; no sooner is the soul made sensible of the mighty redemption, but light, and life, and joy, and peace, appear in the heart through the power of the Holy Spirit. Reader! what saith your experience to these grand concerns? Are you still in bondage and prison-frames to the thousand evils of a fallen Babylonish state; to sin, to diverse lusts, and pleasures; to the alarms of conscience, the fear of death, and a judgment to come? Or hath one like the *Son of man* made you free, and brought you out? Oh! to grace, what mercies do the redeemed owe! And what will they eternally owe when grace is consummated in glory! *Though now, if needs be, they sow in tears, and are in heaviness through manifold temptations, yet are they* *looking forward to the certainty of reaping in joy. These light afflictions, which are but of a moment, are working out for them a far more exceeding, and eternal weight of glory.*¹ (Hawker, Poor Man's Old Testament Commentary: Job-Psalms, 587)

Footnote:
1. 2 Corinthians 4:17.

35

Reading: Malachi 1

"Was not Esau Jacob's brother? saith the Lord: yet I loved Jacob, and I hated Esau." Malachi 1:2-3 (AKJV)

My soul! sit down this evening, and ponder over some few particulars of the characteristics of grace, and behold its freeness, fulness, unexpectedness, greatness, sovereignty, and undeservedness; and yet, if possible, more astonishing than either in its *distinguishing* operations. The Lord himself invites his redeemed people to this blessed study; and when a poor sinner can receive it, and mark his own interest in it, nothing more tends to humble the soul to the dust before God, and compels it to cry out, under a deep sense of it, "Lord, how is it that thou hast manifested thyself to me, and not unto the world?" In this demand of God, the question is decided and answered: "I have loved you, saith the Lord. But ye say, wherein hast thou loved us?" or, as some read it, *Wherefore* hast thou done so, when we were utterly undeserving of it? How is it, Lord, that thy grace was so personally distinguished? To which the Lord replies, "Was not Esau Jacob's brother? yet I loved Jacob, and hated Esau." As if Jehovah had said, I have been pointing out my distinguishing love from the beginning. Was not Esau Jacob's brother; yea, his *elder* brother? And had any right of inheritance arisen by birth, or from my covenant with Abraham, was not Esau before Jacob? Yet to show the freeness and sovereignty of my decrees, before "the children were born, and had done either good or evil," it was said by me, "The elder shall serve the younger."[1] – Lord! help me to bow down under a deep sense of thy sovereignty, and to cry out with the patriarch, "Shall not the Judge of all the earth do right?" or in the precious words of the patriarch's Lord, "Even so, Father, for so it seemed good in thy sight." My soul! sit down, and trace the wonderful subject all the Bible through; and when thou hast done that, ponder over thine own experience, and fall low to the dust of the earth, in token that it is, and ever must be, from the same distinguishing grace alone, that one man differs from another; for all that we have is what we first received. And how marvelous is the distinguishing nature of grace, when passing by *some* that we might think more deserving, to single out others apparently the most worthless and undeserving. The *young man* in the gospel, full of good deeds, and, as he thought, within a step of heaven, shall go away from Christ very sorrowful; while *Paul*, in the midst of his hatred of Jesus, and making havoc of his people, shall be called. Nay, my soul! look not at these only, but look at thyself. Where wert thou, when Jesus passed by and bid thee live? How wast thou engaged, when grace first taught thine eyes to overflow, and He that persuaded *Japheth* to dwell in the tents of *Shem*, persuaded thee, and constrained thee by his love? And what is it now but the same distinguishing love, and grace, and favor, that keeps thee, under all thy wanderings, and coldness, and backslidings, from falling away? Who but Jesus could keep the immortal spark of grace from going out amidst those floods of corruption which arise within? Who but Jesus could prevent the incorruptible seed from being choked forever, which at times seems to be wholly encompassed with weeds, or buried in the rubbish of thy sinful nature? Precious Lord Jesus! let others say what they may, or think what they will, be it my portion to lie low in the deepest self-abasement, under the fullest conviction that it is thy free grace, and not creature desert, which makes all the difference between man and man! Oh! for the teachings of the Holy Spirit, the Comforter, to accompany all my views of this most wonderful subject! And when at any time pride would arise in my heart, on any supposed excellency in me, compared to others, or when beholding the state of the vain or the carnal, oh! for grace to hear that voice speaking and explaining all: "Was not Esau Jacob's brother? saith the Lord; yet I loved Jacob, and Esau have I hated." (Hawker, The Poor Man's Evening Portion, Apr 26)

Footnote:
1. Genesis 25:22-24.

36

Reading: Malachi 2

"For the Lord God of Israel saith, that he hateth putting away."
Malachi 2:16 (AKJV)

And well is it for thee, my soul, that he doth: for if the Lord God of Israel had dealt by thee *once*, as thou hast been dealing with him *always*, thou wouldest have been ruined forever. But what is the cause of thy mercies? Is it not the covenant faithfulness of God thy Father, founded in his own everlasting love, engaged in his promise and his oath, to Jesus, and secured in his blood and righteousness? And is this the cause why the Lord God of Israel hateth putting away? Oh! for grace to see the cause, to adore the mercy; and where the Lord God of Israel rests, there, my soul, do thou rest also! See to it, my soul, that thy life of faith, and thy life of hope, are both founded in Jesus, and not in the sense thou hast of these precious things. The things are the same, how different so ever, at different times, thy view of them may be. The everlasting worth, the everlasting efficacy, of Jesus' blood and righteousness, is always the same; and his people's interest in it the same, although, from the different view we have of it, at different times, it seems as if sometimes it were lost, and our own state was worse and worse. My soul! upon such occasions call to mind this sweet scripture: "The Lord God of Israel saith, that he hateth putting away." Observe, the Lord not only doth hate putting away, but he saith it, that his people may know it, and properly esteem his unchanging love. Oh! to cry out under the assurance of this precious truth, and to feel the blessedness of what the Lord saith by his servant the prophet: "The Lord thy God in the midst of thee is mighty: he will save; he will rejoice over thee with joy, he will rest in his love, he will joy over thee with singing."[1] (Hawker, The Poor Man's Morning Portion, Sep 7)

Footnote:
1. Zephaniah 3:17.

37

Reading: Malachi 3

"*Because I, the Lord, have not changed, you descendants of Jacob have not been destroyed.*" Malachi 3:6

It is no small attainment to be built up in the faithfulness of God. This forms a stable foundation of comfort for the believing soul. Mutability marks everything outside of God. Look into the Church, into the world, into our families, ourselves, what innumerable changes do we see on every hand! A week, one short day, what alterations does it produce! Yet, in the midst of it all, to repose calmly on the unchangeableness, the faithfulness of God. To know that no alterations of time, no earthly changes, affect His faithfulness to His people. And more than this – no changes in them – no unfaithfulness of theirs, causes the slightest change in God. Once a Father, ever a Father; once a Friend, ever a Friend. His providences may change, His heart cannot. He is a God of unchangeable love. The promise He has given, He will fulfil; the covenant He has made, He will observe; the word that has gone out of His mouth, He will not alter. "He cannot deny Himself."[1] Peace then, tried believer!

Are you passing now through the deep waters? Who kept you from sinking when wading through the last?

Who brought you through the last fire? Who supported you under the last cross? Who delivered you out of the last temptation? Was it not God, your covenant God – your faithful, unchangeable God? This God, then, is your God now, and your God forever and ever, and He will be your guide even unto death. (Winslow, Morning Thoughts, Feb 24)

Footnote:
1. 2 Timothy 2:12-13.

38

Reading: Malachi 4

Reader! pause over the solemn, the very solemn and awful account here given of the great and dreadful day of God, so often spoken of in scripture, and so certain and sure. Think how tremendous the judgments which will then overtake the ungodly. *For if the righteous scarcely be saved, where shall the ungodly and the sinner appear.* Oh! what paleness, horror, and everlasting dismay, will then seize every Christless sinner, when appearing before the Judge of all the earth; without an Advocate to plead his cause, and void of all righteousness to justify his person.

Reader! what can I ask for you, or for myself, as a boon from a bountiful God in Christ, but that now, even now, while the day of grace continues, Jesus may arise as the sun of righteousness on our benighted souls, with healing in his wings. Be thou, dearest Lord, our light, our life, our righteousness, now, and forever. Oh! be thou the one great source of our peace, who hast been the confidence and hope of thine Israel; and as thou hast been made a curse for thy people, so may they be made the righteousness of God in thee. Farewell *Malachi!* farewell till meeting together at this great day of God. May it be the portion of both Writer and Reader to meet all the *Malachis* and *Elijahs* of our covenant God in that day, when Jesus shall come to make up his jewels, and amidst the host of Patriarchs, Prophets, and Apostles, to praise God and the Lamb for ever and ever.

And now, Reader, as with this Part of my *Commentary*, I close the sacred volume of the Old Testament scripture, I beg once for all, and finally, and fully, that you will bend the knee in prayer as the author hath done before you, that the Lord will bless all that it contains, as far as it is agreeable to his holy and eternal truths, and pardon all that is amiss, which human weakness, ignorance, and infirmity, have given birth to, in this feeble endeavor to be helpful to the Lord's household. May that sin-bearing Lamb of God, that taketh away the iniquities of our most holy things, cleanse all that is here unholy and unclean. It is my intention, if the Lord favors such a design, to prosecute in the same plain and humble manner, the several Books of the New Testament, by way of Commentary. But this I leave, as I do all other events, bounded as they are within the limits of a life hastening now fast to a close, to Him who fixeth both the time and place of His people's habitation. In the mean season, I here set up my *Ebenezer* afresh. *Hitherto hath the Lord helped!*[1] And concerning my further wishes to write the Commentary for the *New* Testament, as the Lord hath permitted me to finish one on the *Old;* if the gracious Master should say concerning this, as David remarked upon another occasion, *I have no delight in it;* with him I would submissively say, *Behold! here, I am, let him do to me as seemeth him good* Amen.[2] (Hawker, Poor Man's Old Testament Commentary: 1 Kings-Esther, 562–563)

Footnotes:
1. 1 Samuel 7:12.
2. 2 Samuel 15:26.

Works Cited

2017. *Christian Standard Bible.* Nashville, TN: Holman Bible Publisher.

Hawker, Robert. 1808. *Poor Man's Old Testament Commentary: 1 Kings-Esther.* Vol. 3. London: Williams and Smith.

—. 1808. *Poor Man's Old Testament Commentary: Job-Psalms.* Vol. 4. London: Williams and Smith.

—. 1845. *The Poor Man's Evening Portion.* A New Edition. Philadelphia: Thomas Wardle.

—. 1845. *The Poor Man's Morning Portion.* Pittsburg: Robert Carter.

Spurgeon, C. H. 1896. *Morning and Evening: Daily readings.* London: Passmore & Alabaster.

Winslow, Octavius. 1856. *Evening Thoughts.* Leamington, England.

—. 1856. *Morning Thoughts.* Leamington, England.

Robert Hawker (1753–1827):

Robert Hawker, a Royal Marine assistant surgeon, Anglican priest, and author, was born 1753 in Exeter, England. He was married aged 19 to Anna Rains, and they had eight children altogether. He was ordained as a minister in 1779. It was in the pulpit that "the Doctor" was best known and loved. Thousands flocked to hear the "Star of the West" preach when he was in London. An Evangelical, he preached the Bible and proclaimed the love of God. (Wikipedia: Robert Hawker 2020)

Charles H. Spurgeon (1834-1892):

Charles Haddon Spurgeon, an English Particular Baptist preacher and author, was born on 19 June 1834 in Kelvedon, Essex, England. He married Susannah Thompson in 1856 and had twin boys. Spurgeon remains highly influential among Christians of various denominations, among whom he is known as the "Prince of Preachers." (Wikipedia: Charles Spurgeon 2020)

Octavius Winslow (1808-1878):

Octavius Winslow, a pastor and author, was born on 1 August 1808 in Pentonville, a village near London. In 1834 he married Hannah Ann Ring and had ten children with her. He pastored churches in both America and England, spending most of his life in England. He was also known as "The Pilgrim's Companion," and was a prominent 19th-century evangelical preacher in England and America. (Wikipedia: Octavius Winslow 2020)

CPSIA information can be obtained
at www.ICGtesting.com
Printed in the USA
BVHW091755010822
643553BV00003B/47